HOW DO PLANTS GROW?

Botany Book for Kids
Children's Botany Books

BABY PROFESSOR
EDUCATION KIDS

Speedy Publishing LLC
40 E. Main St. #1156
Newark, DE 19711
www.speedypublishing.com
Copyright 2017

In this book, we're going to talk about how plants grow. So, let's get right to it!

Have you ever planted a seed in the ground and watched over the next few days to see when it would pop out? Most seeds are really tiny, but they have within them all the elements needed to create a new plant. Once the conditions are right, the embryo inside the seed starts to germinate. This just means that it pops out of its hard seed casing and starts to grow!

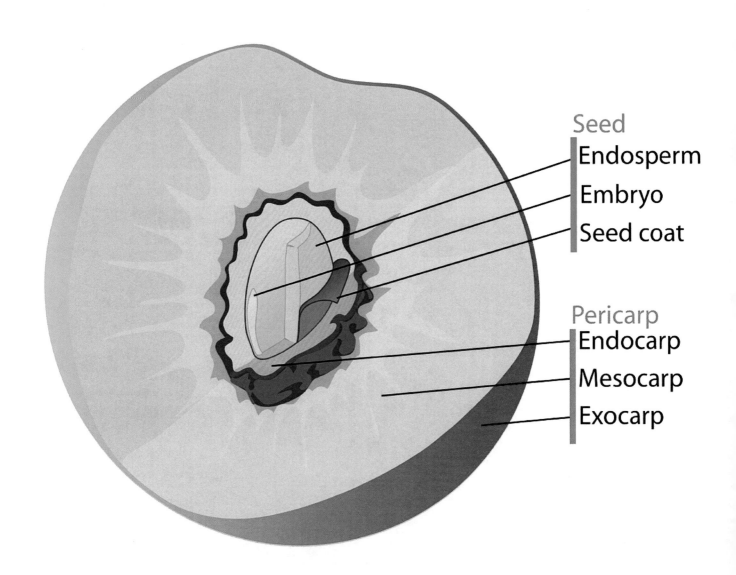

Seed
Endosperm
Embryo
Seed coat

Pericarp
Endocarp
Mesocarp
Exocarp

PARTS OF A SEED

Although the seeds of various types of plants are different, most seeds have three main parts:

- The seed coat or outer shell of the seed
- The endosperm
- The embryo

THE SEED COAT

Some seeds have a very thin coat and others have a very thick coat. Those that have thin seed coats can germinate easily because water and light get in quickly. If you take a lima bean and soak it in water until the next day, you can easily pull off its seed coat with a gentle pull. Have an adult help you look at the seed coat under a microscope.

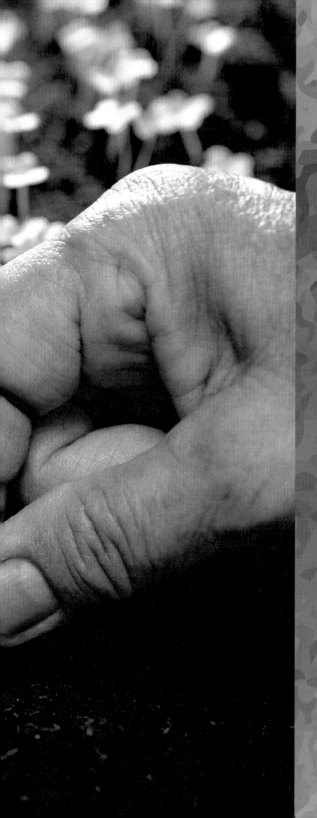

The downside to thin seed coats is that the seed is also more easily damaged. If a seed has a thicker seed coat, it's better protected, and can stay inactive for much longer. Seeds that have thicker seed coats usually get eaten by birds and other animals and then deposited into the soil when they poop. The process of digestion helps break down the tough seed coat and the poop is a fertilizer for the seed.

THE ENDOSPERM

In most seeds, the endosperm is right under the seed coat. It's usually wrapped around the embryo. It provides both starch as well as proteins that are food for the embryo until it sprouts.

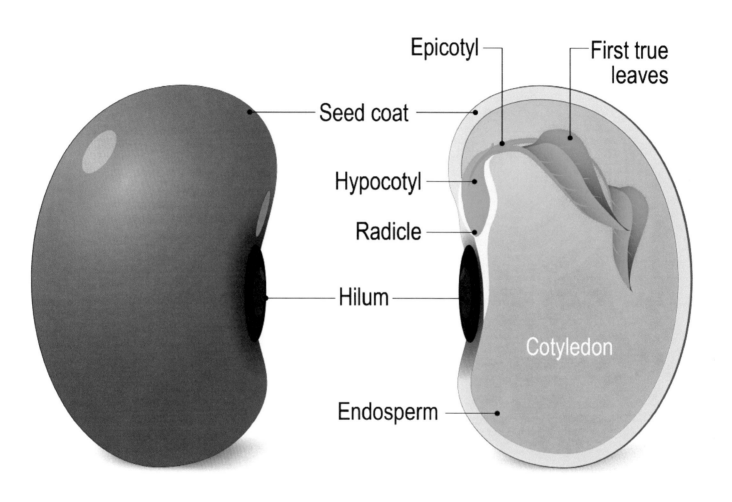

Epicotyl — First true leaves

Seed coat —

Hypocotyl —

Radicle —

Hilum —

Cotyledon

Endosperm —

Outside   **Inside**

White Rice

The endosperms of plants are food for us too! Popcorn and white rice are examples of endosperms that people eat. Shredded coconut is another example of an endosperm. Scientists estimate that about 2/3 of all the calories that humans eat come from plant endosperms!

THE EMBRYO

The embryo is the tiny "baby" plant. It has all the cells that it needs to become an adult plant. The embryo is made up of three major parts:

⇨ The primary roots, which are the first to come out of the seed

⇨ The cotyledon or cotyledons, which help feed the embryo during germination

⇨ The embryonic leaves, which are the first leaves that pop out of the ground when it sprouts

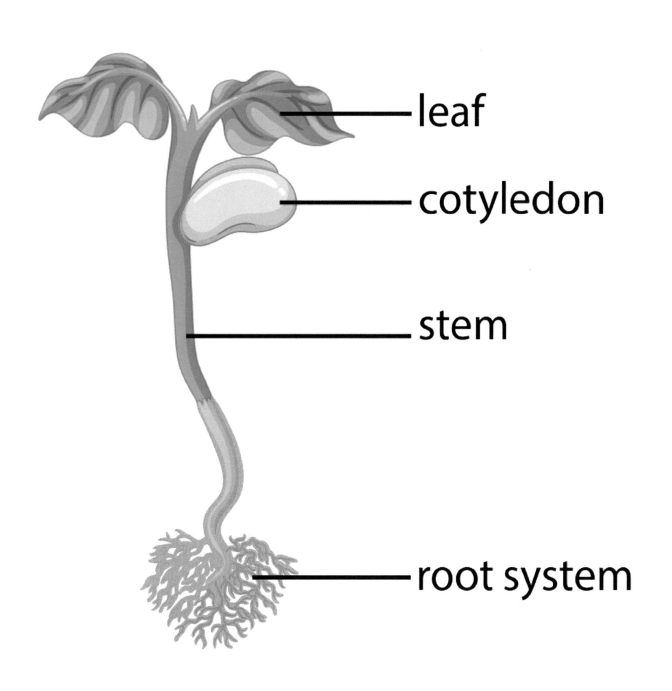

leaf

cotyledon

stem

root system

Monocot

Dicot

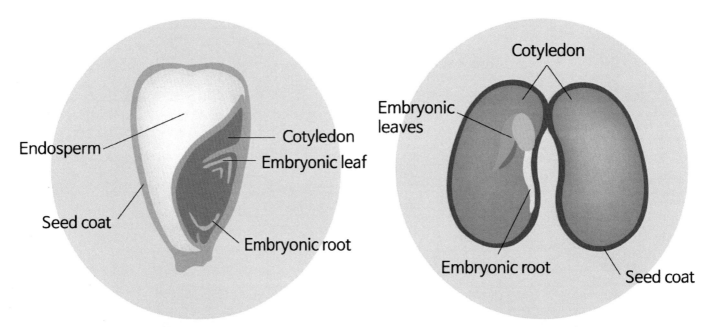

Endosperm

Cotyledon

Embryonic leaf

Seed coat

Embryonic root

Single cotyledon

Cotyledon

Embryonic leaves

Embryonic root

Seed coat

Two cotyledons

Some seeds only have one cotyledon. The plants with these types of seeds are called monocots. Other seeds have two cotyledons. The plants that have two cotyledons in their seeds are called dicots.

Most seeds have to be planted in soil in order to grow. One way this happens is when people plant seeds in their gardens or farms for growing flowers or fruits or vegetables. Sometimes seeds just fall naturally to the ground when a plant withers up or dies.

WHAT HAPPENS WHEN A SEED GERMINATES?

Toucan eating a Guava fruit

Two other ways that seeds can get to fertile soil is when they are scattered by the wind or washed into the soil by water. Animals and birds sometimes eat fruit with seeds and poop them out somewhere on the ground where the seeds can grow.

Once the seed is in a location where it's surrounded by some soil it may germinate. However, some seeds can stay in the ground for a long time without germinating. In fact, in 2005, scientists planted a seed that was about 2,000 years old.

Seed being planted

The seed was dormant and hadn't germinated because it was in an environment that was completely dry. Once they provided the right conditions for it, it began to germinate and eventually it grew into a healthy date plant!

So, how does a seed know when to germinate? If you get some dry seeds from a nursery or gardening store, the seeds haven't started to germinate yet. They're dormant, which simply means that they aren't active. If you add water to them, they will more than likely start coming to life.

Mung Bean plant

In a few days, you'll see their roots start popping out of the shell casings. However, just because the seeds have started to germinate, doesn't mean that they'll grow into healthy adult plants.

Most seeds need three conditions
before they can germinate and
then grow into full-sized plants:

- A source of fresh water
- Fertile soil that has nutrients
  for the new plant
- Enough sunlight to warm the
  soil on a regular basis or an
  artificial light source that
  does the same thing

Fertilizer

WHICH GROWS FIRST THE ROOTS OR THE LEAVES?

The tiny seed is like a survival kit for the plant until it can get the nutrients it needs from the soil. Inside of it, the seed has some food to keep it going until it can make its own food. Once the conditions are good for the seed to germinate, its new tiny roots pop out first.

After the roots grip the soil, it's time for the plant's stalk and its first tiny leaves to come out. It's becoming a sprout! If you planted the seed, you wouldn't be able to see any of this amazing process until the leaves started to push up out of the ground.

Scientists still have things to learn about the process of seed germination. When a seed absorbs water, the food that it has stored inside starts to convert to energy. This energy is in the form of enzymes that begin the process of sending its roots out. Once the roots are working to get nutrients, the enzymes "tell" the stem and leaves to come out too!

DO ALL PLANTS BEGIN LIFE AS SEEDS?

Not all plants start life as seeds. Only plants that have flowers start their lives as seeds. Plants that produce fruits, vegetables, or nuts are all flowering plants. There are other types of non-flowering plants that don't produce seeds at all. For example, moss is a type of plant that doesn't have any flowers. Moss grows from spores.

Moss

Propagation by cuttings

There are other ways for plants to start too. Sometimes you can place a leaf's stem or a section of the stem of the plant into the soil and it will start growing roots and make a new plant. These pieces of the plant that can grow into a new plant are called cuttings. A plant's root system can be used to create new plants too. You can sometimes cut runners or tubers off the root system and place them in fresh soil and start a new plant.

Expert gardeners and scientists know how to take two different plants and join them together to make a new plant. This process is called grafting.

Grafting Cherry tree over a Plum tree

ONCE A SEED GERMINATES, WHAT'S NEXT?

As soon as the first shoot of the plant can be seen at the ground's surface, it's called a sprout. The sprout's roots are getting nutrients from the soil so it can grow bigger. Along with the warm sunlight and the carbon dioxide from the atmosphere, the sprout has all that it needs to grown into an adult plant.

Once the sprout is a tiny plant that has few leaves to spread out in the sun, it's called a seedling. After it gets a few more leaves and is a bit bigger it's a young adult plant. Eventually, it will be a full-sized adult plant that can reproduce by developing flowers.

Sunflower fields during sunset

Flowers of the Strawberry tree

The flowers will change into fruits that contain new seeds. So the stages of the plant life cycle for flowering plants are:

- Seed
- Sprout
- Seedling
- Young adult plant
- Adult plant that can reproduce

As soon as the sprout's leaves are big enough to capture sunlight, it begins the process of photosynthesis. This process, which turns energy from the sunlight into sugars, helps it create the food that it needs to survive.

Green Sprout

SUMMARY

Flowering plants grow from seeds. Seeds need water to germinate and can stay dormant or inactive for a long time if they don't have the proper conditions to germinate. Most seeds germinate when they have three conditions: a source of water, fertile soil, and a source of light that's hot enough to keep the soil warm over a period of time.

The seed is like a "survival kit" that keeps the plant embryo alive until it's ready to germinate. Once the seed germinates, it begins by pushing its first root into the soil. Then its stem and tiny leaves start to break the ground's surface. At that point the seed isn't a seed anymore.

Now it's a sprout! Once the sprout has a small stem and a few leaves, it's called a seedling. Its roots, stems, and leaves will continue to grow until it's a young adult plant. Soon, it will be a full-sized adult plant that can reproduce and eventually create seeds for new plants.

Awesome! Now that you know more about how plants grow, you can find out more about the world of plants in the Baby Professor book The Incredible World of Plants- Cool Facts You Need to Know.

Visit

BABY PROFESSOR
EDUCATION KIDS

www.BabyProfessorBooks.com

to download Free Baby Professor eBooks
and view our catalog of new and exciting
Children's Books

Made in United States
North Haven, CT
20 April 2022

18430424R00038